daughter, while i'm still here

poems by

Marilyn J. Baszczynski

Finishing Line Press
Georgetown, Kentucky

daughter, while i'm still here

ACKNOWLEDGMENTS

Sincere gratitude to Leah Huete de Maines and the editors of Finishing Line
Press for selecting my chapbook for publication. Also, to the editors of the
following journals and anthologies in which these poems first appeared:

"In the Palliative Care Wing" in *Lyrical Iowa*, The Iowa Poetry Association.
"Storytelling at 7:00 a.m." in *The Healing Muse*, 20, no. 1, Fall 2020, SUNY
Upstate Medical University.

"On Burying Mother's Teeth" was included in the directory of the public art
piece, the *Telepoem Booth*, installed in Council Bluffs, IA, Spring 2020. It was
also published in *Conestoga Zen Anthology* (Conestoga Zen Press, 2021).

Publisher: Leah Huete de Maines
Editor: Christen Kincaid
Cover Art: Marilyn J. Baszczynski
Author Photo: Chris L. Baszczynski
Cover Design: Elizabeth Maines McCleavy

Order online: www.finishinglinepress.com
also available on amazon.com

Author inquiries and mail orders:
Finishing Line Press
PO Box 1626
Georgetown, Kentucky 40324
USA

Contents

to mom,
you always will be

forgive me

another bit of advice: take care of your teeth. dentures are no fun, make you feel old, and are easy to lose. my bottom one often bothers me at dinner, food gets underneath like sandy grit. one time i slipped the denture into my napkin, tucked it on my lap. my dining companions didn't notice and i forgot, leaving my rolled-up napkin on the table then went back to my suite. bedtime, two dining room and laundry room searches later, it was found and returned. ugh. embarrassing. losing them and having them.

gleaming perfect teeth
like pearls aligned in pink crown
too painful to wear

daughter, while i'm still here

let's not be broken records,
i've already given too much advice.
enough that you're here.

even as words slip away, we connect
in an umbilical blood to blood sense.
i know your cells,

they carry my message printed
in half your DNA, my blue eyes
and crooked toes.

today you read me poems i inspired—
angry rants about lying, wistful laments
about dead babies and lost loves.

you transcribe my dreams, my gloves,
my hiding. you imagine my backbone
in a tree's gnarled arthritic limbs.

your words wrap me like my quilts
of pink and white roses. your clear
aquamarine eyes take me in.

a laugh rumbles up past congested lungs,
catches in my throat and i cough, while
tears tumble over my crinkled cheeks.

if i were a rose bush,

promise you wouldn't cut my blooms. i'd invite you
to come sit in my garden, enjoy the fragrance,
watch my colors shift with the sun:

blush-golden hybrid teas along the drive,
carmine and crimson floribundas filling the front lawn,
myriad salmony-pink grandifloras out back.

please don't cut them to bring inside. too much work
pruning, spraying, watering, to shorten their flowering
and shrivel, slump, tumble off stems in vases.

those rose bushes are long gone with my move to assisted-living
and now into hospice, and yet you still like to protect me
like a rose. but nothing lasts forever.

all the rose bouquets you gifted me, i kept them until dried
then stored the petals in jars under the bathroom sink. one day
you'll find them, all those years, perfumed and preserved.

rethinking high heels

while we admire my snazzy stilettos
jewel-toned and bejeweled
filling two long shelves
like rows of crayons
waiting sentinels
to escort me
anywhere

before arthritis
crippled my spine
before parkinson's slowed
my steps to a shuffle and made
lifting feet baffling before needing
a walker to get across this bedroom

and yet   soft turquoise leather pumps lure
me like a dear old friend   calling to go out
have some fun   i imagine my grand entry
to the lounge and dining room   ending
in a twist-tumble and broken pelvis

so i put on brown velcro-closure
sensible flats to remind me
of who i can no longer
be   let's be real

i dance better
without
heels

trying to surface

i fall asleep in splashes of fuchsia-turquoise-amber
chiffon floating in a sea of uneven breaths

anxieties forgotten   frown lines soften
borne on waves of stories and songs

i revel in them   dream-dance with your dad
at oktoberfest '63

savor cold beer   clink over plates piled high
with sausages and sauerkraut   wait   i need

to rearrange my hair or brush a stray crumb
from the corner of lips but you grasp

my hand   i strain through the murky waters
of memory back to seize my name and

your happy hello but before i can stop the words
that boy is stealing my clothes

bursts out of my mouth to my confusion and yours
so you hunt and find skirts and pants tucked away

in cupboards and garbage bags and even in the freezer
where's my two-piece pink and white swimsuit with bows

it's missing too   again words i didn't want
didn't realize i was thinking them

you ask if i remember how you tried teaching me to swim
i know how quickly i'll sink when you let go

dream-dance

tonight i sit as always looking
out the bedroom window
     a low rumble and the storm
     spills like a river of black
          ink from clouds that blot out
          the moon and the stars

my steps and breaths are heavy
as i shuffle down the hall
     slip out of my nightgown
     into the opaque dark where
          rain washes coolness over this
          translucent parchment-skin

rinsing my now silver hair
as the smell of earth rises
     wet blades of grass tickle
     the bare soles of my feet
          my white arms stretching
          like branches in violet lightning

i watch my shadow twirl to
the trees' hula-swaying heartbeat
     by 6am i sit inside again
     beside my bedroom window
          the fourth floor nurse
          wonders why my hair is damp

we wade through old photos

me dancing with your dad on the ship,
en route to our promised land;
ugh, such tousled, morning-after hair!

my 22-year-old face in a train window,
dreamy dove flying into the unknown;
what a wind-blown mess.

among family friends gathered at tables
laden with fresh hungarian sausages;
with that kerchief-turban and hair tucked under?

bundled up with ice-storm-houseguests
for an impromptu skating party on glassy roads;
my hair all flattened under a knit cap.

sitting in adirondack chairs on our shady veranda,
we clink icy glasses like glam movie 'dawlings';
the hair again, sweaty and bobby-pinned up.

four cats purring asleep on my lap,
stretched-out-legs-turned-movie-loungers.
i'm wearing face cream and a headband!

you tease me for always wanting to be
dressed up, made up, hair done. but i know
you'll make sure i look pretty when it's time.

not a hallmark moment

i want you to throw them out: all the love letters
and valentines, mementos of a romance
and wedded bliss cut short, even the mother's
day cards going back almost sixty years.
there are three dresser drawers full.

i've kissed them often enough—those x's
he always added under his name, and
the hearts you doodled after yours.
don't look so upset. they were never
meant for you to keep.

sight

i can't open my eyes this morning
too tired / it hurts / don't need to look
i know who you are
a relentless warm washcloth
with soft words wafting
like wispy clouds
my eyes yawn open with a blue
sky of knowing everything about you
i still see all your layers—
chubby baby with downy white hair
giggling at belly raspberry kisses
confident ponytail running ahead
pink plaid skirt swishing
first day of kindergarten
strong teen swinging up on horses
to race bareback across fields
now the retired college
teacher and grandmother—
i can sense your future
i can see you struggle
with emptiness and loss
see you stuff holes with words
and wish i could help

examining x-rays

we study my films together
all black and white like the photos that fill
old albums you now have in your home.

the doctor shows us a series
from the last four years, the last
three weeks, four days ago,
one last night.

the parts that used to be black
and clear now cloudy with ghostly
strings of floating squids, splotches
of baby ones crowding out
the blackness.

jackson pollock might create
a giant canvas and call it
"pneumo-opus no 28 in black and white,"
hang it in a gallery where people,
old and young, can file past
pay their respects.

don't raise your arms, you tell me

i don't want to scare you
it's getting harder and harder to breathe
quick movements bring a dizzy spell
heart medications are failing

breathing is harder and harder
let's watch the wind blow leaves across the yard
i've tried all the heart medications
see those clouds skittering through slate skies

you loved watching wind blow leaves as a child
and thought bare trees shivered in the cold
like slate clouds skittering through skies
isn't asphyxiphobia fear of suffocation

look at the bare trees shivering in the cold
i'm afraid   i can't breathe
i don't want to die by suffocating
relax   breathe with me   this will pass

i'm afraid i can't breathe
it's just a dizzy spell from moving too quickly
this will pass   keep breathing with me
i'm okay i don't want to scare you

linking breath

i remember several times each night
i would tip-toe to the crib railing
peek through white slats
watch your rising and falling chest

i'd stay with you
follow soundless puffs in and out
stroke the feathery white
tufts on your head

i'd hum a lullaby up to the stars
winking at me through the window

today the railing is up on my hospice bed
you reach over to brush white curls
from my forehead and stroke my hand
careful to not disturb the iv line

several times this night i feel you lean close
monitor the rise and fall of my chest
breathing   still breathing
as i hum keeping time

when words fly

i know you're here but i'm busy
reciting poems to put some order
back into the chaos of my head

grab at words floating
in the airspace between us
try to give them weight
anchor them to bedsheets

they won't keep still
we have to follow them
to find the magic

together we throw them high
like little birds they flit away
out of reach until
a few begin to congeal

and call me back home
i have breakfast for you
is this morning's abracadabra

distraction through a hospital window

six stories down past two parking lots,
mist clings like a wet woolen sweater
to willow branches stubbornly gold
against an urban prairie of gray
bare oaks above gray rooftops
in a gray sky.

a distant plane flies over the scene
like a fly creeping across a constable
or turner painting. i wonder if
the insect will turn down towards
spiky trees clustered along the bottom.
i raise one finger to trace its route

but feel your hand warm on mine.
were you sitting here the whole time?
your callused hand grasps my soft
one firmly. i want to tell you
i'm going soon, but not today.
it's too cold and wet.

storytelling at 7:00 a.m.

twice a day, every day, every week, nurses
consign the beating hearts they care for
to the hands of succeeding shifts.

throughout the hospital, they stand in twos,
heads bent, touching sometimes, faces intent,
to share and listen.

they tell each other stories
of people they barely know, yet with intimate
details, corporeal and explicit.

the listeners want to get it right, ask questions,
take notes. it is their charge, to carry the stories
forward and pass them to future listeners,

these carefully prepared parables of pain and hurt,
kidney failures, excretions, healing arteries or dosages
including family help or interference.

a cacophony of narration shivers
along corridors past shushed rooms
where trust waits in curtained beds.

hair-washing and dresses made of sunshine

the nurses washed my hair yesterday.
it flows now in a silver curtain
around my face. i wish

i could rinse it in fresh sunshine
like while walking along the path
to humber creek.

i wish i could lean over the bridge
railing to feed the ducks, feel
the wind in my tresses

tossed in all directions, like bits
of bread crusts i'd scatter
in the rushing water.

today you pamper me, brush my hair,
tell me how beautiful it is,
a ritual of many years.

as sunlight inches across my bed
my thoughts float out aloud:
you should collect enough sunshine

to fill this room then make me
a sunny gown with shooting stars
stitched into the lace.

i laugh at myself, it sounds silly
to say it aloud, but i can imagine
how fine that would be.

if you dream me,

after i die, you can begin
to forget these last weeks
of how i am now.

i will be back with you as i was,
twirl you to the "blue skirt waltz,"
we'll sing "you are my sunshine,"
enjoy our afternoon coffee break.

dream me into birthday parties,
i'll be the one you hear laughing
behind the candles.

dream me into your dances
with my great-granddaughters.
you'll hear my tapping feet,
my voice that background hum.

i'll stroll with you to the pond,
watch the deer on summer evenings,
behind you, in the corner of your eye.

winter solstice

today the sun hangs low; i feel
earth's pivot to where we wait.

mid-afternoon, let's shove away wan sunlight,
i struggle knowing my home is a place

packed up and put away like a dollhouse
banished to the attic.

sundowning, that confusion
at day's end, comes early.

i want to reach up, push graying skies
back, keep this dementia at bay.

this solstice is in my flesh.
i, too of the tides and seasons,

prepare to shift beneath changing light

in the palliative care wing

from the window of this wing, we
watch invisible birds.

they sing sweetly from bare winter branches.
i feel them enter my hours of waiting.

i suffer the clap of their folding wings
and the heat of their breath on my cheek.

i catch glimpses of feathers
in the curvature of my cornea—there,

grazing my shoulder, reflected
in blue iris, a bird's shadow

in the starry snow globe
of an eye. i smile.

a rush of air, a flutter
perhaps, or no,
not yet.

a cinquain, last time

be good to each other / forgive
yourself / never give up / be
happy / take care of your teeth

epilogue

On Burying Mother's Teeth

Two months after the funeral
I find Mom's dentures
in her bathroom cup,
toothbrushes arranged on top
like a headless bouquet.

I can't keep her teeth. I can't give
them away or throw them out.
I take them in a zip-lock baggie,
along with trowel and yellow roses,
to the gravesite.

Well-watered, new sod peels back
like loose lips. I dig down an arm's
length, and like a sneaky, confused
tooth-fairy, implant the package,
replace soil and sod, add the roses
to the headstone's vase of flowers.

No need to fret about losing
your teeth any more, Mom.
We could go to the dining room
for lunch, choose crusty
buns or chewy beef,

while I laugh or cry or try
to swallow a too-large
chunk of grief.

With Thanks

Additional and heartfelt thanks to the poets and friends who have shared in the joys and the trials of the writing of these poems and have provided much caring support: members of Omega Poetry Group and Iowa Poetry Association, especially Shelly Thieman, Dawn Terpstra, Steve Rose, Dennis Maulsby, and Bill Rudolph. A special thanks for the encouragement of Debra Marquart and John Sibley Williams in their inspiring workshops and critiques.

Loving gratitude to my family: to my children and grandchildren for listening to me read my latest poems on the phone or in person to let me know if it "makes sense yet;" I always value your input and your opinions. To my husband, Chris, for convincing me to make the time to put this collection together, and especially to have faith in myself and my writing; this book would not exist without your support. You have my heart, always.

Marilyn J. Baszczynski is a retired French teacher, originally from Ontario, Canada, who lives and writes in rural Iowa. Her chapbook, *Gyuri. A Poem of Wartime Hungary* (Whistling Shade) was published in 2015. Her recent poems appear in *Backchannels, Conestoga Zen Anthology, Flying Dodo, Gyroscope, Halfway Down the Stairs, Healing Muse, KYSO Flash, Last Stanza, Scapegoat Review, Shot Glass, Slippery Elm, Star82 Review,* and *Sunbeams,* among others. Marilyn is editor-in-chief for the Iowa Poetry Association's *Lyrical Iowa* anthology since 2017.